SUNNYSIDE
PRIMARY SCHOOL

NATURE IN CLOSE-UP

# FOOD CHAINS

JAN ETHELBERG

ADAM & CHARLES BLACK    LONDON

## Contents

| | |
|---|---|
| What is a food chain? | 2 |
| The woods | 4 |
| Which animals live on leaves? | 4 |
| Ichneumons and other parasitic insects | 12 |
| The larger animals | 16 |
| The largest animals | 23 |
| When animals die | 23 |
| You and the food chain | 36 |
| Poison in the food chain | 38 |
| Balance in nature | 40 |
| Glossary | 39 |

Published by A & C Black Ltd, 35 Bedford Row, London WC1

First published in this edition 1976. Originally published by Borgens Forlag A/S, Copenhagen, as *Fødekæden*

©1974 Jan Ethelberg and  © 1976 A & C Black Ltd (English edition)

ISBN 0 7136 1634 2

Printed in Great Britain by Colour Craftsmen

The sun heats the earth. Its rays provide the energy for all life on earth.

## What is a food chain?

When an insect grub or larva* eats a leaf, it is part of a food chain. If a bird eats the grub, it too becomes part of the chain: leaf→grub→bird. And if the bird in its turn is caught and eaten, yet another link is made.

The grub and the bird eat to stay alive. So do you. All animals must eat to stay alive.

But what does the leaf live on? Each leaf is like a small factory: it uses air and water to make sugar, on which the plant lives. But as well as air and water, the leaf must have sunlight. The sun is the energy supply for the leaf 'factory'.

Without the sun's energy, nothing could live on earth.

*Words marked like this are explained in the glossary on page 39.

Leaves on trees use the sun's energy to grow.

In autumn the leaves fall.

Earthworms and bacteria* feed on the dead leaves.
Slowly the leaves are broken up and become
leaf mould.

Under the top layer of dead leaves you will find
leaf mould or humus*.

Next spring, new plants will grow through the
leaf mould.

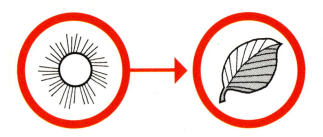

## The woods

In spring, the trees burst into leaf. They use the sunlight and air. Through their roots, the trees take in water and mineral salts which help them to grow all through the summer.

Fruits grow on the trees. When the fruits are ripe, they fall to the ground or open and drop their seeds. In autumn you can find many fruits and seeds on the ground, for example acorns and 'conkers'.

The leaves of many trees now begin to go brown and fall. They settle layer upon layer on the floor of the wood. If you look under the leaves, you will find many small animals—earthworms, woodlice, millipedes, slugs and many insects.

## Which animals live on leaves?

The earthworms eat the dead leaves, but they cannot digest them fully. Worm droppings contain some small remains of leaves. Bacteria now take over and break down what is left. Slowly the leaves turn to 'mould', which is rather like garden compost. The fruits and seeds which dropped to the ground now sprout in the mould, and young plants begin to grow. So the forest uses its own waste, year after year.

Some animals suck the juices out of the leaf. Others eat bits of one leaf, then go on to the next and eat bits of that.

### Gall wasps

Gall wasps are small winged insects. They lay their eggs on leaves. Some gall wasps prefer oak leaves, others prefer beech.

When the larva of a gall wasp comes out of the egg, the leaf grows in a special way to make a little 'house'. The larva then lives inside the house, called a gall, living off the plant juice until it is ready to come out. Plant galls can be many different shapes and colours. If you cut a gall open, you may find the larva still inside.

## Butterflies and moths

Butterflies lay their eggs on leaves. When the larva, which is a caterpillar, hatches out of its egg, it starts to eat the leaf on which it finds itself. Some caterpillars eat many leaves every day, for example the privet hawkmoth. The caterpillars of very small moths eat less than half a leaf in all their life.

An adult moth or butterfly does not eat leaves like a caterpillar. Its mouth has turned into a *proboscis*, a thin tube with which it sucks nectar from flowers. When a butterfly or moth flies, its proboscis is rolled up and hidden under its head.

In spring, a gall wasp laid eggs in an oak bud. Two bud-like galls have formed where there should have been leaves or branches.

*Above left:* These leaf galls were made by a gall wasp.

*Above:* A saw fly larva is eating a path through the leaf

This snail will eat a hole through the leaf.

*Above:* This caterpillar eats the remains of its own egg before it begins to eat the leaf.

*Right:* A large caterpillar like this eats many leaves each day.

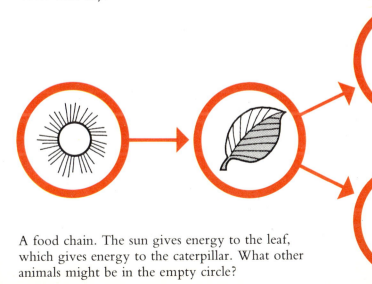

A food chain. The sun gives energy to the leaf, which gives energy to the caterpillar. What other animals might be in the empty circle?

Saw fly larvae have
eaten these leaves.

8

9

*Above left:* A parasitic\* wasp has found a larva in a tree. It sticks its *ovipositor* (which means 'egg-placer') through a crack in the bark and lays an egg on the larva.

*Above:* Ichneumon larvae leave a caterpillar in which they have been living. The ichneumon larvae will develop; the caterpillar will die.

Some ichneumons lay their eggs inside the eggs of other animals. Here a spider's eggs have suffered.

*Above left:* A ladybird hunting greenfly.

*Above:* The larva of a lace-wing fly has caught a greenfly.

A spider has caught an adult lace-wing fly.

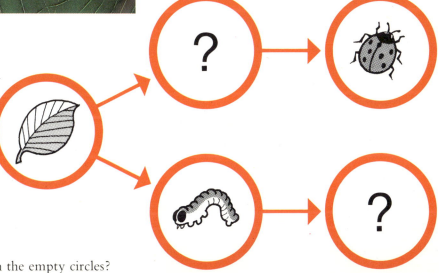

Which animals can be put in the empty circles?

# Ichneumons
# and other parasitic insects

### Saw flies

Saw fly larvae also live on leaves. As they eat their way through the leaves, they make special patterns of holes or stripes. You can tell which kind of saw fly larva has been eating a damaged leaf by the kind of pattern it makes.

Many insect larvae make use of trees and leaves. But while they eat, their enemies lie in wait. Even if they burrow beneath the bark, they are not safe.

### Ichneumons

In summer you can find the big ichneumon fly (big Ophion). It crawls round trees, on the hunt. From time to time it points its ovipositor through a crack. In the photograph of a parasitic wasp on page 10, the ovipositor looks like a black hair-pin, sticking out behind the insect.

If the insect feels a larva underneath the bark, it stays. Then it pushes its eggs through the ovipositor and on to, or even into, the larva. The victim is called a 'host'.

When the eggs hatch, the ichneumon larvae will at once begin to feed on their host.

### Beetles

The ladybird is a beetle which hunts greenfly. Greenfly are found in swarms on plants, sucking plant juice. If a ladybird finds some greenfly, it feasts on them. Ladybirds are very useful to gardeners.

A large fly has caught a smaller fly.

You can clearly see the ovipositor sticking out
behind this ichneumon.

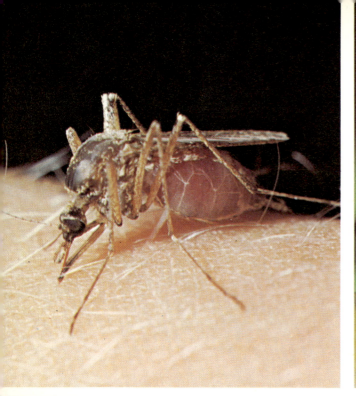

The dragonfly nymph lives in lakes and marshes. Here it uses its strong jaws to crunch up a tadpole.

The dragonfly nymph★ turns into a dragonfly. Here the dragonfly has caught a moth, and hides in the grass to eat it.

*Opposite page*
*Top left:* A mosquito using its proboscis to suck blood from a man's arm.

*Top right:* The fly's proboscis is short and wide.

*Below:* Butterflies and moths have a long proboscis, to reach right down into flowers.

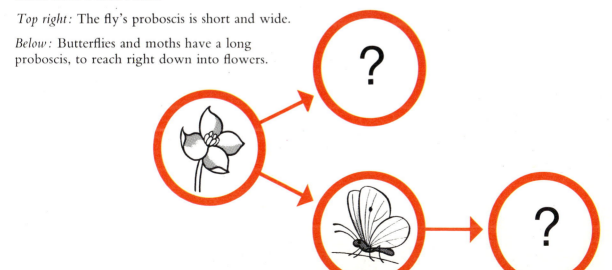

What animals could be put in the empty circles?

# The larger animals

## Amphibians and reptiles

Newts and frogs feed on animals. In water they eat daphnia and other water fleas, as well as the larvae of insects. On land they hunt earthworms and insect larvae.

Lizards may catch small dragonflies, but mostly they hunt flies and larvae which they catch in the grass.

Grass snakes eat many frogs, but also newts, lizards and fish. They always swallow their prey live. Vipers, which paralyse their prey with venom before eating it, live on mice and sand lizards.

## Birds

Sparrows and songbirds live on seeds, grains and insects. Blackbirds live mainly on seeds and berries, but while they are feeding their young they also catch earthworms and beetle larvae.

Swallows live on insects which they catch as they fly. You may have seen how they dive and dart to catch mosquitoes over ponds and water-meadows.

Gulls eat almost anything—food scraps, dead animals, fish, worms, insect larvae.

## Mammals

Moles and shrews eat only insects and larvae in the soil. The hedgehog eats insects, earthworms and slugs, but also windfall fruit.

Voles eat the bark off trees, as well as fruits and berries. Field voles cause damage to crops by eating grain.

Which animals could you put in the empty circles?

These birds are looking for earthworms and beetle larvae in a newly ploughed field.

Many birds eat berries.

This young swallow is begging for food.

In the sea there are many food chains. Predatory* fish, such as shark and cod, eat smaller
fish. The smaller fish, such as herrings, eat small
animals, such as shrimps, crayfish and water
fleas. And these small animals in their turn eat
plankton. Plankton consists of very tiny plants
and animals which float in the water. The
smaller fish are also hunted by birds, such as the
seagull in the photograph.

Which animal could be put in the last circle?

*Above left:* The owl hunts by night. Both kestrel and owl are 'birds of prey', which means that they eat live animals.

*Above:* The kestrel hunts during the day. It lives on insect larvae, earthworms and field voles.

This shrew is hunting insect larvae. It cannot hear the owl cruising quietly towards it.

*Above:* Cats hunt mice and moles.

*Above right:* The mouse is killed and eaten quickly, if the cat is hungry.

A fox will eat almost anything—dead animals, food scraps, insect larvae, beetles, lizards, mice or birds.

This is the story of a bird of prey. It has eaten three smaller birds. Each of these, in its turn, had eaten three caterpillars which had eaten three leaves.

# The largest animals

The smaller animals have many enemies. The large animals, especially the big predators, have few enemies or none.

From the diagram, you can see that many small animals and leaves are needed to feed one bird of prey.

## Birds of prey

Buzzards, kestrels and peregrine falcons hunt their prey by day. The common buzzard circles above the fields, watching for mice, but the kestrel can hover quite still in the air, keeping its eye on everything that moves in the field below. It hunts mice, but also larvae and lizards.

The peregrine falcon is one of the fastest birds in the world. It catches other smaller birds in mid-air. It eats mice and rats too, and every now and then it will swoop on a hare.

When the peregrine falcon sees a bird flying below it, it folds its wings, plummets down at almost 300 km/h (about 180 mph) and seizes the bird. Its sharp claws close on the bird and kill it immediately.

Owls hunt at night, flying quietly and then pouncing on their prey. Owls eat rats, shrews and birds, as well as mice. Owl pellets can be found on the woodland floor. The pellet contains the remains of food which the owl could not digest.

## Other meat-eaters

Foxes live almost everywhere, in fields, in woods and even in towns. But you rarely see them because they hunt at night.

Foxes annoy farmers because they hunt chickens, ducks and geese. But foxes can be useful because they do control the number of mice. If there are too many foxes, they have to be killed.

# When animals die

All animals die sooner or later—but you don't see many dead animals. Most are quickly eaten by gulls, crows and carrion beetles, and what is left is attacked by bacteria and turned into mould.

Leaves, dead plants and dead animals all rot and help to form mould. In that way all the materials which make up living things are used over and over again.

It has been raining. Here comes an earthworm.

A frog sees it.

The frog eats the worm.

A grass snake sees the frog.

Gulp!

The frog disappears.

25

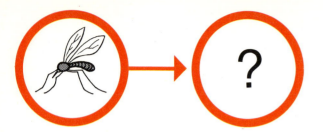

Some animals catch their prey in the air. Which animals can be placed in the empty circle?

Look for other food chains in the air.

This is just one of many food chains found among the leaves and branches.

Can you find other food chains in the trees?

This food chain takes place in fresh water. Which fish could be placed in the empty circle?

Can you find other food chains in water?

Which animal can be placed in the empty circle?

Try to find other food chains on land.

26

This lake is near a wood and has fields and marshy land around it. Many different animals live here.

In the drawings you will find the animals. Many of them fit into the empty circles earlier in the book.

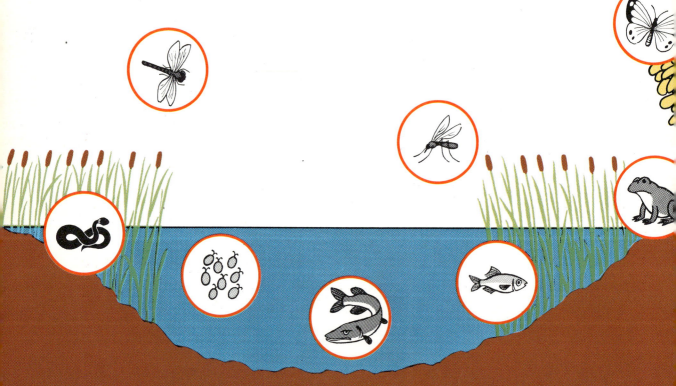

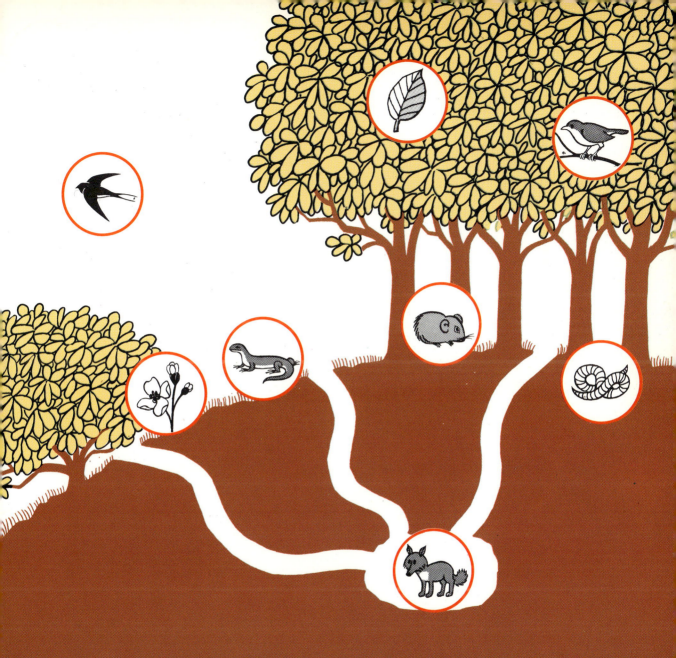

A wasp uses its jaws to gnaw wood to make its nest. You can see the strong jaws on this wasp's head.

A bird of prey has a sharp beak. It uses it to kill and tear its prey to pieces.

Animals protect themselves in many ways. This larva looks like a twig. This is one method of camouflage★.

If a bird seizes a lizard by the tail, the lizard escapes because its tail drops off.

31

Some animals protect themselves by their colouring. This is another method of camouflage.

The newt is well protected on muddy land—if he keeps absolutely still. Predators notice moving things.

Spiders have two poison fangs, which they use to paralyse their prey. Then they can eat in peace.

When summer is past, it turns colder and there is less food—fewer leaves, fewer larvae, and so on. The swallows flock together before setting off for warmer lands where they can find food again.

It is winter by the same lake. Many animals hibernate★. They have eaten well before starting their winter sleep.

But many birds still live in the open, as there are still berries on some bushes and trees.

Here is a food chain you know. The hen eats grain.

Then it lays eggs.

## You and the food chain

What do you eat and drink in a day?
Can you draw some food chains which include you?

Many millions of people must have food every day, so we build our own food chains by farming. The photographs show just one example: grain → hen → egg → human being.

But not all eggs are used for food. Some are allowed to hatch. Some of the chickens are killed for you to eat. Others are left to grow up. They turn into hens which in turn lay eggs.

The eggs are collected and sold in the shops.

And we buy and eat the eggs.

Many food chains involve people. What could be put in the empty circle?

# Poison in the food chain

Vast amounts of grain are needed to feed farm animals, and for making flour. But some grain is used for sowing, to produce new plants.

The grain can be protected against fungi by treatment with mercury. The mercury treatment is very poisonous, and kills all the harmful fungi.

But what happens if the poisonous grain is used, by accident, for animal feed instead of for sowing? The poisonous mercury travels from link to link of the food chain. Finally it could poison both animals and people.

Look at the drawing on page 22. It is the diagram of a food chain which starts with some leaves and ends with a bird of prey. If the leaves are sprayed with poison, each leaf receives so little poison that it is not harmed.

But if each caterpillar eats three poisonous leaves and each of the smaller birds eats three poisoned caterpillars, the bird of prey receives the poison off 27 poisonous leaves.

The last link in the food chain receives most poison. Sometimes it can be us.

Here is the food chain again. This time the hens have eaten poisonous grain. The poison travels up the chain until it reaches the human being.

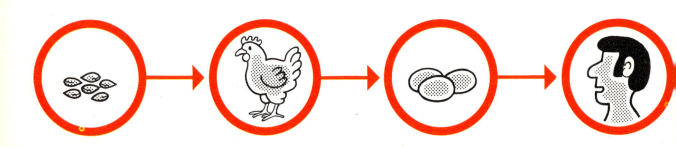

38

# Glossary

**bacteria**    very very tiny plants of one cell which use dead plants and animal matter and cause it to rot.

**camouflage**    special colouring or shape which helps an animal blend in with its surroundings so that it cannot easily be seen.

**hibernate**    to hide away and sleep throughout the winter.

**humus**    small particles of decayed plant and animal material.

**ichneumon**    kind of insect whose larva is parasitic on or in other animals.

**larva**    a larva develops from an egg and looks quite unlike the adult insect into which it will develop. The stages in the life of most insects are: egg—larva—pupa—adult. Caterpillars, maggots and grubs are larvae, which eventually become butterflies, moths, flies, mosquitoes, etc.

**nymph**    a larva which gradually changes into an adult insect without going through the pupal stage, e.g. dragonfly.

**parasitic**    a parasite is an animal which lives in or on another plant or animal, depending on it for life, but giving back nothing in return. Tapeworms are parasites which live in the stomach of other animals. Some plants too are parasites.

**predatory**    predators hunt other animals for food.

This picture shows the basic things we and other animals need to stay alive:
sunlight, air, water and green leaves.

## Balance in nature

Nature keeps its own balance. We human beings can disturb the balance by throwing waste and poisons into the natural system, for example by spraying crops without thinking of what might happen.

At the same time, all farming interferes with the food balance. We have to interfere if there is to be food for us all. It is a huge problem to provide extra food for the growing number of people in the world, without damaging the balance of nature beyond repair.